# LONG DIVISION

**UNIVERSITY OF CALGARY**
Press

# LONG
# DIVISION

## Gil McElroy

Brave & Brilliant Series
ISSN 2371-7238 (Print) ISSN 2371-7246 (Online)

© 2020 Gil McElroy

University of Calgary Press
2500 University Drive NW
Calgary, Alberta
Canada T2N 1N4
press.ucalgary.ca

LIBRARY AND ARCHIVES CANADA CATALOGUING IN PUBLICATION

Title: Long division / Gil McElroy.
Names: McElroy, Gil, author.
Series: Brave & brilliant series ; no. 15.
Description: Series statement: Brave & brilliant series ; no. 15 | Poems.
Identifiers: Canadiana (print) 20200226266 | Canadiana (ebook) 20200226274
   | ISBN 9781773851310 (softcover) | ISBN 9781773851327 (PDF) | ISBN
   9781773851334 (EPUB) | ISBN 9781773851341 (Kindle)
Classification: LCC PS8575.E47 L56 2020 | DDC C811/.54—dc23

The University of Calgary Press acknowledges the support of the Government of Alberta through the Alberta Media Fund for our publications. We acknowledge the financial support of the Government of Canada. We acknowledge the financial support of the Canada Council for the Arts for our publishing program.

Printed and bound in Canada by Marquis
♻ This book is printed on Lynx Opaque Ultra paper

Copyediting by Helen Hajnoczky
Cover: Gil McElroy, *Moon on a Long Thin Wire #2, Colborne, Ontario,* 2019,
   digital photograph
Cover design, page design, and typesetting by Melina Cusano

*For Ernestine Amilie Justine Kircher McElroy*

# 1

# TWENTIETH

*I have so many excellent reasons to lose myself*

PAUL ELUARD

## Desnos

I've dreamed
there enough, which is to say that
I've dreamed of becoming accustomed, folding
back around to
so much
that what it has could very well,
oh…

I've dreamed
of me swayed
by you, face
& lips I've dreamed of so.
I have so often
stilled time so often,
fit the contour & for days
weighed wakening appearances.
I could have.
The shadows
were longer, then.
Sleep & all the time sentiment
ruled.

Kiss that.

---

*My Desnos conducts illumination. He is a giver of shadows.*
*My Desnos is seen best at night, adventuring in it.*
*Splashed with mud, my Desnos shivers at the dawn.*
*My Desnos insists on a heart in all its form.*
*My Desnos gazes in my direction, vibrating with typhoid.*
*My Desnos is never 46.*

## Apollinaire

You're
in Europe. You're
tired, & you're
reading poetry all day. You're
very pompous
& still confessing a
hole here, a world
there, a heart, a
wretched heart.

Goodbye
life. Wherever you go I'm sick of hearing
me.

---

*Apollinare is the best example: undemanding Apollinaire,
inevitable Apollinaire, Apollinare with all the answers.
You saw yourself in Apollinaire, Apollinaire in your eyes.
Look behind me, Apollinaire, while I mourn.*

## Breton

On my lips this

You see me, immense

Once again, my eyes anywhere at all

Sand, darling, there inside them

They're helping despair

Don't stop. My neck is defined by blood

I was

I was

Despair, what despair

With green kinds of things

The towel

My hands, in succession

---

*I'm braving Breton. I need to.*
*At night I'm Breton. I'm waiting for Breton, the arboreal Breton*
*dressed by priests.*
*In my sleep I see Breton in the trees.*
*Breton will be everything I've ever lost.*
*Breton will be drawing a crowd, Breton all alone.*

*Breton you notice.*
*Breton is passing by.*

## Reverdy

To understand the room
the eyes must flow. The eyes
themselves tremble. The ear
is far too late.

Cheeks slide around such faces.

I want
a livid shadow
that holds me
by the head. Your head
rises too high out of sheer
astonishment. There's
wind on your lips
pale in the distance. It
won't last if it's
too windy.

In the next room
I listen. I wait. My memory
is emptying itself.

Your eyes.

Your cheek.

___

*Reverdy's talking Reverdy's methods.*
*Reverdy's rapture.*
*Reverdy's ten fingers.*
*Reverdy's pale sadness.*

*Reverdy's remorse.*
*Reverdy's last harvests.*
*Reverdy's luminous cures.*
*Reverdy's rough murmurs & terrible thighs.*
*Reverdy's jealous flanks.*
*Reverdy's heart at the very last moment.*
*Reverdy's hands I can't believe.*
*Reverdy's other movements into remorse.*
*Reverdy's calls you couldn't hear.*
*Look under Reverdy.*
*Who will praise Reverdy?*
*Reverdy's a long way off.*

## Eluard

It
radiates aloud. Pleasures
think about it, sorrow
loves it. In the shadows
dreams caress it, generous
& light & dazzled
with clouds.

It
goes its own way. It
has its makeshift reasons that old loves
efface. Day to night
entwines in its clouds.

Your name
is burnt-out of it
in storm & unbounded daylight.
Besides this, your neck is involved. Your
frozen first name, too.

Tomorrow it
turns out
well.

---

*You know, Eluard has feet.*
*You know, Eluard has arms, & hands held behind his back. But*
*I have not imagined them.*
*I have not imagined that Eluard has pleasant fingertips.*
*I keep Eluard in front of me.*
*I keep Eluard fully lit.*

*I keep Eluard to the flame.*
*I watch Eluard burn.*

## Tzara

Days in my head.

Promises of arms.

There's only your beautiful hair no one can name.

You promise
clarity without quarter. But my heart
empties itself
to the stars. My fingers
grieve, then
entangle with your lips, your
smile, your
handkerchief.

Yes, it's you, your
brightness, your
whole & entire hands.

---

*This is why I am not Tzara: there is little or no Tzara.*
*But I totally believe in Tzara, the newborn Tzara, the waltzing*
*Tzara, the no-name Tzara.*
*Laughter & lots & lots of Tzara.*
*Weighty Tzara.*
*Tzara on the lips.*
*Tzara, like a slap on the face.*
*To hell with Tzara.*

## Aragon

Wednesday it happened.

Cushy foreskins, suddenly.

Her breasts

      His marriage

*broom broom*

Here's what you paid for: gulled maps & the navy of God. But good heavens, it's madness! There's darkness in all directions!

To me my heart is foreign to me.

---

*When I think of Aragon, I remember a heap of stones.*
*As for Aragon, my opinion won't stop the future or any other.*

*But when I think of Aragon, my tongue becomes confidential.*
*As for Aragon, he doesn't understand.*

*But when I think of Aragon, his grandeur weakens his gentleness.*
*As for Aragon, his voice rings in my ears.*

*But when I think of Argon, the light shades other walls.*
*As for Aragon, he stays hidden in a tree that the sun passes by.*

*But when I think of Aragon, sympathies follow me from the darkness.*

*As for Aragon, I congratulate his wholesome smell.*

*But when I think of Aragon, if I were alone I would refuse to leave the shadows.*
*As for Aragon, what company!*

*But when I think of Aragon unleashed, the excessive heat is really experienced.*
*As for Aragon, he doesn't understand.*

*But when I think of Aragon waiting, his sharp teeth ease the itching.*
*As for Aragon unleashed, what a pity.*

## Funny Guy (Picabia)

Having to make
daguerreotypes around me
because I am not rich without
knowing it…

Heaven to find
in a cloud, but,
alas, it's only your hair, vibrating with
explications.

A dream
should cure me, a sock in
one's pocket that turns
into salmon outfits.

That's that. In
lowercase.

---

*The last thing I want is Picabia.*
*There are lines around the Picabia attraction.*
*Picabia sees my friends – the kind of friends who make you*
*forget Picabia – & then aims & shoots.*
*Last night Picabia almost poisoned me.*
*Think of Picabia's face, overheated Picabia.*
*There are a thousand Picabias.*
*Picabias are always free.*
*I don't have a single Picabia.*

# 2

# I/O:
# A COLBORNE PSALTER
# (01 − 23)

[01] O
who has not
stood, or
sat, night
& day

nor
paced beside a stream *a creek, a spring, a rising land*
*away from lake*

*subdued and sundered by highway, caught*

*between such & same* ,

the wind & judgement

dying out

⁰²You
let me be,
gracious & long
in your heart

You
have given,
& I, I
shall lie down,
here


trembling *like grass. Corn*
*a sea waist-high in places. Orchards gnarled with young fruit, & chickens roaming free, strutting*

*& scratching in the narrow between barn & road almost underwheel as I pull up*

*to the mailbox*


asking

³ Consider
me, because
you will

you will &
I shall

my mouth,
broken *with what destruction makes: what*
 *the house that oversaw the lakeshore quarry*
*& the rail tracks doubled between, with what*
*one day whole was next utterly gone but for what*
*dirty gray footprint*
*of concrete*

04 O,
I said,
O, because
I have *O, the trials*

& because I have, I
shall

I
shall melt, sorely
vanish

vex'd

my
eyes gone
away from me, the wedge of tempers grown
old.

<sup>05</sup> Be
gracious & know
this, the
seasons loosed from
troubles, the
regions *Memory. Not fully memory, no, but not risk either. Totally I would with it, with*
*a thing with feathers surprising me surprising it.*

*With*

*a sweep of wing, the not goes on, valued*

*differently*

of
bread
eye-high:

My mouth
is tight & hard-
rimmed

When I cry
on my bed, be
silent

[06] It
had to be
wanted *A place of rates & flawed settlement. Wooden-lidded well found*

*rotten beneath a thin layer of soil & grass, large enough for a child to plunge through. Afternoon shudder*

*of quarry blast*


*& O, every ratio thereof*


Since
the eye minds,
keep us
in the days
of dowsed contours, all true
& such

Our own
by us
is the night

⁰⁷ Why

the lines puzzled,
asking why
I was asking
why

You have
the barbed affection
at hand
& I
not

& when I, I
shall fear, who *For my name, who are they?*

will clean
me?

⁰⁸ Listen
to us,
who, guided,
wait, re-
collecting
our vital
heat

who, waking,
shall clear away the branches
& so see
up, toward the full
Moon *Its freezing of concentrations*

who will
sound

who will
hear

who will
feed you/who will
fill you
up, open,
up

09 I have
taken off
my hands

I have
let go

I have
listened


In a moment, open
your *The great is to me. I begin behind my steps* mouth

¹⁰ Wash me,
to prove
I was
born

Sprinkle me,
& my bones
will steady
me

Do not
give me back
the moveable views *Foolish I, not lifting shed door clear. Thoughtless I,*
*head vs. the door's inertial steel beam. I*

*the acceleration. I*

*the pain & shifted thoughts*


*& O, all I*

*the months of distortion*


Save me
from my
tongue

"I
have visited,
& I have
seen

I
have remembered,
& I have
thought

They
that hunt me,
they shall be
stopped – by my bed *Hardly historical*
shall be
stopped

weary
& without
water

[12] The lake

&

the hills

the running in
the middle

break

burn

be *the zoological first, owl – Great Gray - in headlights, flushed*
*from highway curve in wintry pre-dawn, only then*
*the anthropic I, trembling west.*

quiet

[13] I said
I will

I will

Living like
a ghost *behaving in dark corners*

My time

my tears

& the number
of nothing

[14]Do
not, & they *Six turkey vultures, one*
*dead rabbit, &*

*the mathematics of feeding I*

*interrupt*

will


because
I was young
& would not
wait

¹⁵ Give
& in-
cline
things that
we will not
hide

In
the sight
of land, in
the daytime, split
rocks, make *cool, hard desire*
streams

[16] They have, but
I never *self-electrified & with nothing to do but ever*

*even*

The furrows
were just, the
withered grass like
rope in the fields

In these arms
no one
stays

[17] They have
looked on
because they
are strong
like *Like atoms, after all*

the hands
over my mouth

¹⁸ When I
was dappled
& everything before
my eyes
scorned

choosing *chair (kitchen) for want of a ladder (step). The clothesline's cedar terminus*
*& feeding black-capped chickadees untroubled by my presence. The suddenness*
*of wings towards me*

*hawk in close pursuit of another thing with feathers*

*wings brush my face*

*on towards the garage, doubling back, then*
*a hard left down the driveway & away*
*& over*

*Cumulative suddennesses*

*Finding*
*hawk in tree where driveway ends, gripping*
*the failure of bark* the fire

[19] What
things, O what
good
things

My trust
is every mo-
ment given
me

Make
the words by
my breath *Durations, proper intervals, rituals of hesitation, a comet*
*hanging heavy In the night sky*

*its nimble nearness*

*& a name, O,*

*its life breathed in,*

*its vowels breathed out,*

*a light, beseeched*

their
hot & cold
qualifications

broken

bringing

[20] Patience,
more &
more – the
numbers of
them since I was
young

Troubles
& *a sense of tedious baggage* adversities
from the deep places
of the earth
& more
do me
harm

[21] I am,
merely, &
I am,
shaken

I
can count: a few drops of water *Hanging laundry, the sun
haloed & dogged (parahelia, though only one, the eastern such). Mostly the cold
crystallizes such concentration. Mostly*, melted
wax, clay shards
in the dirt…

I am
all of my bones I can count
in the grave

[22] Do you
in deed, so that
it does
not

Spare each
evening, that we may flee *Motley skates, & so forth*
to it

& portion out
the balance

²³ The
ruthless, they
have not
& all

for you, for
they, with
one mind *Distant black dance rising & falling thru dry winter air, acute parabola*
*of crow outrage. Abandoned telephone pole set lone in field, now capped white. A*

*Barn Owl eyeing corn stubble below*

*seeking small verbs beneath the snow, focused*

*& oblivious to the angry adjective above.*

*The concentration*

     *The secondary nouns*

        *Eventually,*

*hawks*

like chaff blown

then
murmured

# 3

# ORDINARY TIME:
# THE MERTON LAKE PROPERS

*Let me say this before rain becomes a utility that they
can plan and distribute for money.*

THOMAS MERTON
"RAIN AND THE RHINOCEROS"

## Proper 30

*S*

Acts,
like one core
mountain

*M*

one revealed, one
mountain revealed
like

*T*

mountains

like

*W*

[…]

*T*

[…]

*F*

like

*S*

terrible saints. Steeping them in the storm. There will be a wind. There will be something marvelous half-buried in the south – & unexpected. There will be combat, after all. Ridge directions stare down at an even place & the dry moments forming there. Thought out three simple glances. Was a bit dizzy at the bad taste left in my mouth. Thought them out again. Chewed them splendid. Then cut them back.

Rainy boots. Nothing thought of while some news resolved. Probably hopeless. Lively ideas feel me, of course. "Hope so," I said at the end, me so pious & anathema. It all strikes me dutiful & such. The morning is competent with sermons dug up for everything. All that, & no doubt then. One gets between symbols, & then kapow!

By night, of course. But enough light dawned. Brick winds large around everything. The road out of places. A couple of thousand snowy silences along the way walking.

The wilderness terribly becomes, now. Sick of it. Mornings I wake up of it. Heavy rain in back of it. It will be too late of it. The lake of of it. I did not return to the right, getting back of it. Each remembered dream let go of it. Really lamentable, but purely mechanical. The 20$^{th}$ century gone astray of it. Very, perhaps. I cannot be sure.

## Proper 31

S

There it all was, as if tired out: countless recognitions fixed
away, spiritless by the woodshed with the sound of perfect
sleeves just outside. My eyes were successful, thinking of the
rain, worrying about my health.

About four, by evening. Quite a bit of it (the dark stuff) after
dinner settled down, into & seen here. But tomorrow isn't
saying yet, then gets back into the snow, cozy except for the
wind & the night. Overcome by grace which was sent me & all
the weight of modern air.

Some seem with such scandalous, useless things, & the
cushions of middle-money (sorrow just so damn lucrative).
Some seem boned, the air low & dirty. Changing colours in
an expanding universe, I think, neatens nothing. There's a
slight haze in the trees rather than the open spaces. It ought
to be futile. It ought to be immutable, hushed & shining.
We've passed through all the security one is supposed to think
about.

& now the houses roar up. Their infernal buzz. Yesterday, it
was all the humming. Outside, a summit of crows & texts I
agreed with. The blessed heads of small ideas.

I am not lost & luminous. Whatever the inert ways of
redemption, even if everything every-time time weakens, the
night is still photographs.

*M*

Be quiet. Someone's shooting. A fine view of brown woolen caps & pines through the short evening light. What is important, though, is the knit-covered mind. The forest disturbs it. Me, I must seem brilliant.

The mountains are ramshackle, every boulder small & virtually monastic. & the yellows are immediately obvious. I've a lot to say about optics. I am clearly of my own tradition, a body of knowing not unpronounceable at such great distances. Cease its saying, though. Cease as long as possible. Be free of its eclipses.

Morning was written in block letters in the tall trees almost as big as people. Yesterday's great views were apparently non-answerable. Petulance & formality came out of it all.

Grace given is a greater grace than grace chosen because of all the circumstances. As to the beautiful outside, the polls say otherwise. Soon, the dismal. Other machines, though, will be glad to have us. At this point, complete mixtures make sounder judgments about things.

Four o'clock. A crowing. The east can be heard. A comet this morning, just only at light. Only excerpts of it, though, through the clouds, foreshadowing something the coming nights I think I am capable of. Really there & pure.

A stage, obviously, its effect & purity I'm just realizing. In a book, years ago, in pencil to the last detail beyond the lines.

Another thing/one thing more: the force of silent streaks of night when you breathed in the stars.

*T*

The reason whether told me. Imagine, I was trying the results. Testing them. I was a fool, see. Such impertinent questions, see. After all or not, I assumed one-thing answers, no choice between choices. Sitting back in September, even if I could have, place as anything settled on seemed certain of mercy.

But when what to say, & where? Learn to write for the telling. I am rushing at one, words to be with it. It is more than I can take it. Relief without shame. Fie upon me! It's all beginning to leak out. It does not couple into the new. Everything more so. Worst, who knew? I may refuse my smallness. I must.

Tell me again. Punch & endorse. Disengage from all the hissing.

Some little snow, now. Powerfully icy hills out there. The facts of fact. Unfaithful gifts. I have renouncing in mind, hot tears, & that one-thing reality eating its way through the snow. But we have each other's grasp. A world of a world of love.

Stove evenings (the other ones just plain silly this time of year). For three weeks now, the good things of the stars. Limitations clear for whom the dying us. But moments in their isolation unite us. & see? Today was good to pass over, right? I had a bright, sunny day & a vast view, bigger than very solid afternoon, above all. Mountains would have worked too. Or ideas of rope. The way in me every way trying a lot. I cannot quite understand months. This evening in the moonlight, the stars opening into.

*W*

Every limitation is clear for the dying us. But moment: common to all the same many us is all that stuff beyond words. Do not want.

Old fashioned struggles would've wrecked us, like, totally. Writings, once they become statements, could complain about it all too enough. Obviously it would upset everybody with problems. Too much to say, see.

Rain was this morning cold (& will still at bedtime). Riches began to appear between them brief. First, I saw beautiful horizons watched under the comet sky. I saw them in the extreme. How could they not be radical? Not as often, apparently, as they should. I saw them as quite bright, like a sky pointing downward for an hour & a half. Rang my bell. Flashed across. Blinked across. My joy.

I feel the need of foul austerity, but everything cannot cope with such a script. Saturday places. I hope to finish the end of November with claims to one in my area. Its aura of true religion. One or two, maybe.


*T*

It is now. No one doubts it. This is no longer comfortable. It's grim, maybe. The world is terrified. One knows that. I, of all people.

Dark mornings will happen. But most of them are known & enhanced rather than what I meant.

Above the word & just to its left there is division. It is seemed. It is built-upon, a complete misunderstanding of. The word misses to the right. The worded regions of the world are unthinkable, their face & welcoming hand just on the brink. Tents, jeeps, & the smiles of all raised up together. Clerical feelings. Smiles everywhere. Habits & the drum of the sun.

Man the pumps. The ambitious constantly miscalculate. They are shadows.

The whole of the day it rained. The day before I got evening. The other ones do too. I must still have some hope. Inexorable, n'est ce pas? Tonight's all about the good things & stars, for some three weeks now. After that, the lamp, for long periods.

Laughter in the woodshed, but one course of its technology was more than enough. A bright, hard pole of light. & really new, too! This is one. The others – the sun & the moon – should be available. Even by starlight, perhaps of all. Perhaps this again, at last.


*F*

Red sky cold morning, but the sun came up crows. Sat outside, all white & frosty. As usual, except for my feet.

Was tempted to a house that was small enough to understand I must be afraid of. & yet I acted. The whole vote so damn tucky. Such trouble! How solid my shifting! It is useless, such troubled & meaningless ground.

Reading is a basic sin I visited after dinner, disturbing thing that I am. Have done with it, though, craving a God under the appearance of craving a god. Necessarily wrong things, but what a lot of fuss, the noises & days becoming tragic words or two. I want out of words – *any* – for weeks. Is terrible to be such a sign of absurdity, but in three of these things a man (sic) might stand there, existing in the bush & in the wood.

28 cold grey days. A week or so ago like tomorrow. 75 sermons. Dismantled professions, & liked them.

After a long hard bunch of benches, restoring the restorations. There will be possibilities. Some copies, too. Shakers would be stricter, & want to make it sounder. But perhaps we realize vested interests acceptable to all.

Woe to nothing before we eat. The modern unfulfillment. The terror thing. Swallow to keep boredom induced. Buy another bottle.


*S*

My lot of questions about silence & passions & observances & so on. I asked to be a topic. Perhaps I should not be. Still, it's a form of religion, final or not.

It's very warm before dawn. High clouds, thin, sweeping roads of. The first minutes tranquil, arresting all the evening din. Had heard drums, then, & some witticisms that quickly became crowded.  Monday morning is a sound place. Sunday morning finished off at the cost of many stamps.

Yesterday, yes, cross-eyed, shiny, & stained with faded red flowers & slate blue skies, shacks, kids & dusty carpets. My opinions – looked for them.

Doing nothing, of course, a possible course. Stopping precisely too an option. Things stirred me, though, stuff tonight I'm going to read (one or two a week, though).

Continued business. Off to its religion, & don't I know good from bad. But willing, I, to let demands all have their free way with me. Will eventually have to this stop, though, or at least reasonably settle down. One is compelled to separate mores more precisely.

Yet what of it? The reality in exaggeration part & parcel. A clear life. Definite. It has to be clear.

## Proper 32

*S*

My week in chapters. 'Ready read very much, & yet all of a sudden seemed kinds of ideas ago, all a week old, least.

The present, one way or another one. Translations of are all mistakes & of a whole spate of mocking styles. It's really not political at all, not at all. I like it terse, see, & not parroting a part just so. Can't escape involvement, I. Pervades the whole see of the world, says nothing but opposition of & to. God knows what giving goes on there ! Don't expect really getting close, I. Uselessly done, I. Yet dissatisfied in town, I. As to typing, just let it die.

Sun out (finally). The morning seemed to sit up all night. A bit premature for yesterday, but today there are interludes, are there not? If I had, I would've been in, would've. Real maps & all, I used to think. Now, a greater grace to die, I. & yet natural things I wish for are beautifully twisted at a rate I never seen before. So it is all still beautiful & marvelously mine, their letters all about the way they are. They are not bitter.

*M*

Because of the appeared for
Because of the idea of dignity for
Because today I remember for
Because also today I remember yesterday for
Because for the first time practical gods imported something for
Because the reason act is done for

Because to me, I had read of it for
Because to me, the mystery of the view begins to degenerate for
Because I know this concretely for
Because the explanation or nothing for
Because as far as seeing goes, I was drunk with all of that for
Because of little impatiences for
Because diversity tires me out for
Because my tongue is tied for
Because it seems to me that words are hopeless for
Because at first sight, perhaps for
Because there, or because they hurt for
Because the hard discipline of for
Because I also shamed for
Because I wish I wished for
Because I wish I knew for
Because the stones have no ideas for
Because the stories found out for
Because of goodness knows what for
Because of all my appetites for
Because reading, among other things for
Because night is occupied for
Because the warm sun appears for
Because my body hurts
Because of the pattern for
Because this morning my glasses were forgotten for
Because I was not aware that it might be for
Because of this afternoon for
Because of my mind for
Because you know it for
Because for

*T*

This morning I'll survey the conservation of problems. So swear I. Yesterday you might've appreciated it, right? I try, & then realize such, see. The whole thing is so freaking ambiguous I've come to this point. The worst situations. & days of such remembrances.

Hence, I tell others to get the hell refuted – but in a way I after all do not abandon. So I come giving equal terms. I give a humble, you see. This begins with love so trusting, if I do this.

& then war.

That was so simple! But it's a sad day, horribly burned of things. Am so disturbed, I. All this thought of things thought of. Sometimes a wish to cut off all of it. Yes, all of it. Need nought but a light & comforting supper. Where is that now?

It has been unusually cold of late. Gotten used to the stars loosened up in the sky, cold. That world heals my soul in moments like these. I arbitrarily find myself. Tell myself probabilities, & perhaps even thinkable ones because of anything I stand for becoming. Coming to dawn I drive out the tranquil, me, building din, hearing drums. Then get lost. Or maybe before.

*W*

Cool, my clear afternoon. Now, can be much more elaborate about it. Bound to be plenty of living. 'Course, it's silly to get lost, right?

Walked the field today. The other end of June was trying to tell me, but was explainless. What would've been. Might've. Could've.

Here, bad words stretched open. Like high mountains. Or clouds in the dark. I had to get out. Yesterday's values half-used, & their uniforms sure didn't help. Wise but naked sterility had a reason, & it wasn't any prettier than its virtues.

A wreath. A group. A handshake. A cutting. A receiving. A beauty.

All these vagaries, a good combination of. I have old age too, probably. Saw a shooting star. Read its entrails without cracking up. But once not nearly enough.

Impatience over nothing natural. Must muster more courage with all that fear of things out & about. Need take care of all the consequences, I. But then the utter madness of coughs. Today, or perhaps not. Remedies are for whomever.

Going over the self to try & get somewhere. Been a bit imagining, too, then becoming, in turn, words. What I will believe, I myself? Well, a need, in the first place. Is this wanted at the heart? It gets away with abandon. But anyway…


*T*


Letting go all speech. This stupid quiet, the burden of. Still thinking, I, of letters. Impossible messages. Voids, even, & their signs.

This morning incapacitated, I look like something weeping. For long times, even. Such trouble. The comet above looked very well. Its practical life the wrong kind, though. Incessant.

My texts insist of me. I do not. Finished up a plan. It is the feast of the plan itself, several days recitative. Yesterday, it seemed clear. Atmospheric, even. Then a man's [sic] body in my own, or should be. A bond of charity, really.

The first time I was thirteen one thing led to another. A giant all year, bound & determined. It was a demanded lie, in effect. There used to be giants. There used to be superstitions exercised. There used to be heads cut off.

Anyway, dead men (sic), earthy & clustered. They are by fact, but out of them, nothing. No whistles. No tones. No hymns of praise, No going crazy.  It jars.

I often wonder, me, wonder between the eyes tears flow out of.

Last night's hours. Dinner & all the lights. Too-bright lights. Talk silenced, final. Stayed down under the window. Good blankets hastily rounded up. Tonight back for more.


*F*

Today will have everything – *everything* – & I think it will have to be done. I'm glad that it will be done. I think anything could be.

Yesterday passed at night, sort of austere & obviously in solitude. I'd been up on its character, in moonlight at the window surrounded by my own rules. Had more than enough dawn, I, clear & overlooked, all scratched-up with tension. I continue my shimmying.

Working me. Little gestures with my arms. In the afternoon will be sorts of exhortations. Some are kinda neat. Some of them swagger. Some of them get out fast, hitchhiking.

It will be good & warm with all the signs of the distance. Absentee counties. Decisions without difficulty. Where's my conscience? By the way, I have nothing but things I have not concerned about. From my body, prestige, hostile or shaking, ready to rate. Or rather.

The mercy of the impossible.

Rain will sweep the day. Come wind. I ought to be content to the end of my rope & the things ignored afterwards. Gymnastics of the real remain, rethought. Was about dry rooms, in various instances. Gone to be, or thought of. Done in the end. 'Lightful day causes a thousand houses, but them of more light cause to leave.


S


Pleasant hill down I continue, onward. Can't stand of it. Complete with forlornness. Even at dinner. Grey skies, like effects. Problems of my own part. Things that are a lot of good.

Often a valley often fallen short of emotion, of denial. The utter loneliness, windy conversions of. Today it is aesthetic but for all my cleverness. Always this nothing – always this hymn, that hymn… I too upon the wall, doing, hear no answer. It is juggling this form, going on here. But a trying place.

Obviously there is that, the very actions I already stuck with. Values too, they clung. I stand & then stand on. There is the sincerity of things. & there is faith. Everything else is views all hidden, implied façades. Jeez, I have feet with fewer givens.

Today, surprise! Important, that one, & powerless to appear compelled. Was going to point it out. Was going to occasion so much more. Truth a mess announced, just sitting there. What a wreck! Perhaps there is nothing external. It is one of hope, mine. Again, look to take the, to be the, heart of emphasis.

It is a ladder, like. This picture visits, right or wrong. I have kept my mouth put down. It is placid. This told, & a truth is somehow woven with the name of my wakening, like. Saw inside the whole.

Weather this morning, though I was not. It suggests nothing of the world if I read things halfway. The other day someone sent me looked pretty damn good. The rest but back at me. I am with hesitation, with anxiety, & am to be commended.

## Proper 33

S

So I am the chief things I put my fingers into. I put myself into everything, all things, & walk on my own feet. Mistrust goes on down there, though.

Not anymore with it, though. I give myself things. I want the hard things. I want the things that travel on & on. If you blame me, it will only burn in my heart.

Ah, such clarity yesterday, just past three. It was very quiet. Started out early with cold, my knuckles drowning out the din. Off I went, my neck with beard. All sorts of ground agreed with my feet. Got lost on it (that's life). The cold broke in the sun. After that, in my room this morning felt better.

This is not completely realized. Today morning I saw the meteors, & they was more exciting than experience. Good as seeing pictures. Better, even, because they just are! The big fat stuff like that is lovely, but I think it doesn't do. The worlds in writing can't be the same. Good & like things. Today may sound wonderful, but I want nothing of it. The more I between the dread, the more visible.

Twenty sorrows. Not the sorrows possible but the sorrows done. They appear only if I am not to obey, as I do, underneath them. Marching would be more intelligent, taking my belly & leaving.

It's a little too much to last. Not something to adjust, I, however much the objective & only star I see.

*M*

Pray for the dead. Witness those of profound mercy. Today replace them.

About my dreams, I'm not sure. Have a shot at such. One must turn away, see, as though peering through any such demands. Concentrate on the pictures. The pictures demand, see. Unmoved by pictures? Well, there are situations, caricatures of. To renounce might be helpful, not to go into dangerous detail.

The stars constellate above, somewhere between good & evil. Yesterday had been summoned. Felt rather hard about it, I. Today there are cardinals for all of us, a lot of scarlet in the cold. Mice. Some wrens.

The horizon red. There'll be rain bickering beautiful & pure tomorrow, cleaning the week. It frightens just a little I can hardly doubt. This is auspicious. By chance such times, all turned inside out.

Cold loneliness, afternoons of having such. My anguished view of the hills. Suffering under such contexts. Yesterday & its values went up in smoke. Affection too. Fine, camera-shy cruelties in the woods. Why did I go there? Spite, maybe.

Today meets me by the door. None of it is not something unimaginable.

On being tired of clouds: walk the length of them. Then turn back. On being tired of the view: note the objections. The fog hides a variety of sins. Back that moment. Work quickly to include it. Then return, wrapped in a blanket.

The deep quiet is terribly gashed with daydreams. The sun gets higher. Lower after morning. The rest for supper.


*T*


Today reached me & so forth just after night. Today it rained, though not some way given out all alike. Stuff lapping at my front door. It's all in some respect, a revered way starting up at quite a pace & trying hard to get my goat, it.

My conclusion too high & tidy. Ugly, even. & another bright thing: I have few pictures & even fewer concrete proposals can't in conscience talk about. Don't think significance. Don't think poses a problem. Don't know how to here the things. But I'll all of it effectively.

The day well watered & meaning, but black & white begun. Cassiopeia earnest then, even. The chance of letters – M or W – at the time. Which? Up, down? It is of what emptiness & strange mores? Midst it, my blood (red), my wound (shin).

Rain on. Thin warmth. Beyond both, I, shivery, true at any length. Yesterday – very cold – had much more to it. Something to do with my hands. Well, no. The blessing of hard thoughts blocked everything. Today's cardinals auspicious, though. A lot of remarks & pictures of such flighty words, all the combines of. A mouse with a neutral face. A few more wrens. & unforgivable me.


*W*


The good, painfully. Sorrow ever be possible. Confession suppressed.

Wondering how it would all fail. No fun, & after all, so real.

Struggling awake, I have wonder. Wonder about motives.
Write them down. Devote myself to hope.

The unfamiliarity. The fear. & to myself every day.

I beg risks, to cease to be. I have acts, accordingly, & that's all.
Broken. Renounced.  The hills I have defiled all gone away.

This is to be. Everything & never will be.

Minutes by the window. Last night in white, now clean of frost
& moon. I see no snow from the window.

My quarrel with the sun. There is another side of I cannot talk,
somewhere out there playing out with what I saw, I. Illusion.
Illusions. Sting of lovely blue. Later cannot be entered just yet.
It's not recognizable just yet. There is no asking it just yet. No
threshold. No end of sorrow. There is this world, undestroyed
just yet.

The window speaks. Light flowers. A period of value, its own
shape. My light. Clouds going on for hours half-revealed.
One who does not is not seen. Testaments without end end.
Afternoon questions. Long truths of time we use for indoor
non-answers – more in my life. Patterns of sounds hear a little
of. Distances in small chords.

At the end a hard summer, a state of grace must come.
Something alive & pure. Even more obviously, the transition
from, uttered all around. Could be expected, but nevertheless
terrible. Wonder more horrible than fair. The loudness, of
course. An utterly painful ear, but only at all. So much noise.

Rackets yet to resign. I went. I thought. I poked at, too. Found a small quiet. Tasted it. Mild.

The same again tomorrow.

*T*

Solemn yesterday. All my great pain died. Yesterday is a distant relative, gave me away alive. Only later tempts to do. All kinds of final pity.

Grounds I cannot account for. What I got felt shaken by my own foolish & absurd strength, resignation to ease, sorrow, & anything else. But I have grace – learned from this, made change. I can see. I can clarify. Validate, so to speak. Useful, so to speak.

Lucid day. Will have it to give, I. Even my tragedy is another thing, & more intensely. A way begins far from necessity, makes me thirst. A collective why? Around my neck some good, some today things. The big too – that comes from things.

Here is another expression in with the others. This time, the stuff. Wings, next. & old brick walls hopelessly without character. Minds with a kind of secure savor. What they cost, the straight pretenses? Cost the dark hours, desperately.

Outside morning. Hidden birds, dismal sun, wildly mistaken butterfly. My feet, those of the left & right, are deeply suspect. Obvious one on side. The whole thing exploited. Crows crow. The afternoon bloods on, causes no joy.

*F*

How glad, from one heart. Clarity in the main thing, but noise in the other half coming along. Across the valley there is much almost out of sight.

Praying, first of all, for the meaning of the middle before one knows how it all comes out. Most me do, & bring it upon myself. The meaning of this something sometimes worth.

Yesterday simply stupid. Simply preferred, I go on. Am mixed up, I. But will soon sleep long sleeps past the very ancient sun. Take where how it deeply dawned.

Alone to the dentist days ago. Esoteric & voracious teeth. Edifying, even. Some imitation of, anyway. After that, came down, me. An anatomy of dissolution waiting in the dark. Less thought, less speed. Jawful pain still.

Voice gone. Respective value of me, too. Its course my interest, nice'n hard. On the valley slope ice & immunity from life. All the radiances of. Very that I have some mention it of. Matter of all, what it means. A lot of again. Fine. Nauseated up, me, or I wouldn't have mentioned it. What nobody knows is what doesn't bore. Ah, crap!

Manner is the limit, & then a lot of it. That's high praise, it is, the thing already dated.

This is a shiny new guess.

*S*

After the rain, sleep. Now, though, frost observed coming back in, the inexhaustibly weak sun mucking about with the thickening morning. Small textures, nevertheless light & incomparable with inattention. In fact, utterly inadequate.

Did I write this? Am singing with attention, I. One of evasion, if worthlessly. Gets me such fussiness of rain & frost. My cold autumnal tongue. Witty cough drops I don't even like.

Begun. Albeit, that seemed such before. Begun again with simple entrenchings in their own right, maybe. Begun its proverbial beheading. Such delight, taking note of things about full! Then withdrawal just like this, ornamented with these, mine bad knees. Anyway, something to retreat with & from. Right?

No lights in the dark. Respectably pitch-dark it was. A big dark – amplified, even. Conditional celebrations held in. Very good. It was good, instead of just touching. Nothing starry about it, though. Cool, more & more. Sore reason brighted right out of me. A grip on my own flatulence only. Pent up. Secure. No running amok.

See? Hidden behind such beautiful gases in their own right such as ones one explodes with delusion, if oiled just a little differently.

Laughed. Finally laughed.

## Proper 34

*S*

This eye I scratched. Insertion, I think. Hard to get at, but I did make a response. There are such minor quests. There are roles over & done, such this need, & after them, life. These things they will hardly will not be determined. The soft embraces of, perhaps, realized.

I must be: essential
 gentle
 never seeing
 necessary
 realized
 faulted, circling secrets 'round me. To me this is necessary, yes. Realized, too, yet that I leave here. Adjusting it, especially so. I really failed, here, really failed. Supposing to worry – it is very supposing, very broken. It is, & it was. I can. I would have. I am. I still will.

I know most of this stuff, know stuff you could see'n feel. Details, though, offend well-borrowed words, remarks I make. All they say is that such stuff is so that it seems. Same kind of trouble, you know. Same talk found to rise in mine life. It means more, gets to be in me. But there will be others – at all costs, others. A past for that we did not ask. We did not ask. We asked nothing in these: the heart, the soul.

Bewildered by snow. Is a little, now. In the whole, though, large. Time to do things. Discuss the pronouns.

*M*

In the night the moon, the south feeling of snow, great &
swooping. Whatever this is, it wears on. There is a light
outside, loaned me. An hour later, another. Enormous day. No
question of its own awful life.

I like making coffee, me, waiting for such, not tense. Do feel
fit, I, fully ordered, full of slow facts & guided eminently.
Ordered. Yes. In so far a ways, arriving at. Like the other day,
its wings mostly melodic. I went out – not too much rain
for that, then. Smoke, though, that might've been related to
something which I have nevertheless forgotten. The other day:
sang it on a stone, I, low & torn.

I guess I got staunched. The sense of a wound got back before
sorrow wedged in. A vague sense of me, yes, & it is always the
same: the air is cold, there is no which which does not belong
to me, the poverty is not beautiful & quiet…

I renounce all my own. Can so, utterly unruffled but not so
safe in restlessness, even if it were. Beaten else as much. The
combination of horrors & stuff when I discovered that. The
great & great let loose. Events they was & most certainly were,
supposed of real strength.

I tend, I. It seems good, the quality & habits of, which is very
fine. Under times locked, pressed in, decided upon. They are
done in private.

The weather most stubborn. & miles from me.

*T*

All day it felt. At noon, surprisingly so. Amazed at it behind me, its brightness at the threshold because of the light. & because of the light, the clarity. The air at least twenty feet high, & the much lighter evening still open, silly & amazed.

Those days when I was whole, most, & fluent – well, they bite me now. Gazing at them now, there in the sun. Keeping on talking to the trees. Reliable them, not like the narrative deer to I spoke, robbed of all the contrary.

Tomorrow to the hills I commit to. Last evening recently slaughtered. All of yesterday, also. Have often skipped going forward, I. Count myself in opposition, refusing wholly, without a light or much use of.

One long, & the others shorter. Hundreds of them. So many other things at arms length. One is, one thinks, but only so far as the sincerity lasts. Then time comes without taking it away. Sobriety all tucked down. The events around me & with me otherwise. I gave. I talked too much. Made glib, even. A knack, I think.

Long stretches between heaven & earth blended by stars like smoke. Will probably try to talk about it. No. Shalt not.  Shall shock the usual silliness out, no less all the routine.

The field is comforting. The whole place surrounded with all things in bits & pieces. It's one way, to me, to high-velocity tomorrow. Ask me how close.

*W*

Rain rains down, rains in a way that just has to be simpled.
Bland & signatureless, the drops left. & radically so. Good
ones necessarily so. Sworn, even.

A week ago's bitter ending now a week ago. Laid out then, I
scarcely knew about my pockets so soonly parodied.

The stars broke off, not looking at all, night all so sober &
serious. Self-importantly behesting, even, the uses made of
them taking of me humiliated moments standing about (&
other stuff that was equally iffy & precisely non-apt). Knew all
along, me. Did not like the fancy bits at the end, though.

Next door, morning coming on. Caught yesterday a great
unknown world known for sure in mystery, in the dark. Once
again, though, overwhelmed by it. Different from hardness.
Good, but longer.

Marched into the bitterness. Lamented at the walls. Disliked
things can still exist, see, still ring a bell, still fall down
amongst dead leaves so tawdry & thin.

Too much rain for that? Distances low & torn flying mostly
about in the stormed distance? Weather styles. Bah!

6 A.M. stars, the hottest known – that kind of thing nothing
against, I. Summer coming again & again, though. So shiny &
bright, gilded & halting.

*T*

Ever, nothing can change. Evening, last. That dusk was done for, presumably. Midnight rolled in. Brutal wind rising. Had some tea, most likely toward the beginning end of it, approximately. Strong, dark, & there, then the sky-is-clean stars' entirely spacious world.

Baby senses, the many names of. I know twelve. Affable. The nicest things.

But before finds me, back in the light, this full Saturday morning's wind running hard while I write this, me. Much more I do not know. Writing in silence. Waiting, all rough & buzzy. Standing back, even. Confusion of constellations I cannot see. The unseen form of shadows in scattered but dignified groups. One, two, three… Oodles more.

Couldn't think of much the other end of last month. All those sentences, especially now that one detested by so many others. One, it would, you'd think, break to some extent. The price of the whole of. One senses this sentence. I must. But why should I? What I am I am, though not as long as possibly, could I. Waiting, yes, but waiting too I spent a great part of, you know. Maybe horrified the good reasons, even. Yes?

Today of this year doesn't want of last night's wasted words. It wouldn't, you know. Its moods of ways never come again. But the wonder! The door. The deserted desk. My buttons. Postcard picture. A letter. Such gifts! Such flattery! Ever enough, the notes not heard, the remarkable sections…

Can always argue, I. This minute a hawk in the wind. Red tailed. I with awe.

*F*

Friday. Bunch of roads. Heavy places. Time & a lot of trees.

Can comprehend it, still, & beaten at that. It must be terrible, such persisting. My own place to walk not even healthy, even. Capturing bricks without mercy.

No one can cry out without mercy. Misery makes a noise. Terrible cutting up. The trouble of such stone & rubbish.

My foot-sense of geography, my instinct by steps. A tough one, alright. At least if a bit snowy. But when I got two conflicted steps forward, another was waiting. The next were absurd, so finally I walked out, me. While I still am & is, do I have?

Stupidity, & totally so. A virtue in me. Will get you nothing but anguish, some of it big. Has always a problem. Maybe tough. May be a lot, without preferences. May be not the worlds that disturbed the idea that it would be a good notion. The thing going ever!

Rushed back into my head. Look, that was relevant, the idea in the middle, not the variety, none of that. Some sign came up, crazy corrugations of. Unconcern goes on ahead a couple of silences. Shaped by holes, me.

The bells last night again. Advent again, the facts of stopping myself. The waited question again. A sense of the view – anyone knows?

Never cease, they tell me. Early mornings behind the little clouds when I had nothing to say among all the nuisances. What I wanted was in the fields.

Yesterday satisfied at the last minute, earnestly & no longer me.


*S*


Follies, the flights into. Almost everywhere, them, when the chairs are comfortable, anyway.

Went quietly muffled, I, though less still. An attack of sentiments in the dark, the moon somewhere out there, Orion downtown & for some reason sharp. Humourless I, & vigorously so. I had forgotten nothing. Nothing!

Watching day build its curious letterings & funny suggestions. Like dinner & a movie. Some talk. & maybe adventures, the merits of. Glad to hear. I went back, me. Took the liberty of my face to others but not to myself – not to one so good.

This is not plenty, though. The life in another way so completely discovered, marvelous for one there. Suddenly, well, suddenly thought in or about my own mind. Preached it, talking things I have no idea of. Under the cedars, me, after dinner, smoldering.

Perhaps deepest after all, yes? Seem trite, taken as a little portion of. Found the ashes of humility beneath some persevering snow. I could see my heart, wet snow ruining it. Went out, scolded thus. Walked to get attached to it, I. The usual trees & branches. Moon doggie, even, I got with the naked eye. Faint aroma of scruples & a liturgical year.

Am I making plain? Cannot say such words again. I still can't see. The hand means, see. No doubts, damaged & overheated as they are.

Get out thems that drives me. Curve over.

Silent. Icy. Hastened across in the long darkness. In the air. In the merest possibility of. In goodness.

The morning here & there. Over it all a roof.

## Proper 35

*S*

The weather comes in character. Grey, this time. & windy.
What seems to be a fact can get so. Am dubious, briefly.
Down, too. Feelings of persistence, still.

Wind woken night path through the snow, space suddenly hit
hard. Where is the meaning of it – on the ground, in the snow,
lit from within? To stand back, to do so, centers on something.
No capacity to go to the shining west. Not to be especially
put off yet again. Quite decent, in a way. Enabling, even. The
Advent thing, again.

I lost my whole heart, me. So misgiving, so badly pulled.
Repugnance doing really well. Or so alleged. Practicing some
supposed things. Dashing. So hot. & taller now, too, routed on
the way to accepting so.

A house on account of its windows must be without harm.
Behind glass one must be come by, lighted up by the problems
we all agree heave up. The trues have enough reasons. Not one
as well as me, though. All know this. Trying to see what to
be angry at. Was of many others. Good & honest should be,
but don't seem so. Autumn zeal, you know. The remedy part.
Complete parts. The simplest been, even every time. Their
fragrances long problems far away.

How very yesterday of me! Always thinking, etc. All this not
to see, not to where I must, me, in spite thereof. There there.
No use where, no perhaps in spite of the good. Some ways
hurt, perhaps sweetly so.

& yet, & in, a deep so anguished with fancy we must be
ashamed of.

Awaiting I go, wild & quiet.


*M*

[…]

*T*

[…]

*W*

[…]

*T*

[…]

*F*

[…]

*S*

[…]

# 4

# THE DOXOLOGIES

*(Some Julian Days)*

Some sort
of afternoon. The heat
will soon be
at home
in its touches. There will be
balanced ones, & other ones
resolved in flames, & then
the sky we will be awaiting like this
will become
really rather
dear.

Do not go
away. Do not go
heavy, tired
of something in
this moment that's going one mile west
of somewhere one mile east. Simple
attentions call, you know, a
garden of days here
in the long now.

*2456629*

I've got
vertigo, & am
seven hours
out of miles but
for a foot.

All overlaps
all, doubt
filling in the simplest ways
of hard horizontals time
sorrowed. There's
one law of rule – one
basic law – for the vast collection
of day.

I can
feel sturdy. I can
assign with my eye. I can
dissolve between one place
out of necessity
to the other.

Dust, more or less.

*2456631*

Oh, the,
the oxygen
of the thin, plastic
future. I feel
the from above
silence. I feel
heat. I feel
rising where wanting is an intervening
small construction of a sun
on the longest but for one
day. The,
the thickness of it
papers the whereby seconds
because the stars fable with
more democratic stuff.

Seriously, though, we
need this anatomy of
sweet little nothings, &
all the balsa-wood nights we can
possibly get.

Put
your thumb out
into the wind.

Waaay out.

*2456632*

What
a fall. Its
almost ignored atoms
left me tired,
mired in dismay with mawkish threats
to my throat. But
it's over & gone – done, kaput –
& another world grown up in my hands,
now. Things
sorta match. The calendar
continues. The roads
are in orderly context. Though
summer has been asked after, I've
new responses to
the intervening of small, almost-
cornfields, &
to the Moon, too.

These
are these, my
unaffected eyes, which
what has been in
the always – a
series of
many of them, anyways – a
halo of ratios rather than
clouds.

*2456633*

Going, going,
& gone. There've been
no exceptions, no
needful buffer of names. Listen
for all the things withdrawn
from you. Listen
for their distant murmurs, if you wish,
off behaving badly in some
dark corner.

We might espouse
the long, shaggy now
& its dubious indoor sensibilities. We might even
choose the navels & doubtful allegiances
of tomorrow's vulgar oranges.

Or we might choose light.

Jupiter rises.
The Pleiades howl.
Stars are falling into the trees.

Call home.

*2456634*

Now, by
bit, I will that
by means of words
my tongue turn to risk
wonder.

Unsayable spoonfuls of sun
compel me to. It's
an ancient pain, an
unwanted haven of
often messy squinting I can
accept. I can
still feel sturdy, &, yes, I can
still assign
with my eye.

The old is not
difficult to who is so remedied,
thin on their feet. There's nothing
in the normal heart but
genuine wounds, durations of agains
& agains, particulate migraines,
& occasional mosquitoes.

You have thirty days.

*2456648*

The start
of the late long, the
new getting
consequent on
barefoot minutes that, gotten,
could. Each week becomes
more palpable than
the last.

Or
not. Moments might
contradict out,
mimicking the style of tons of things so mellow they
might jiggle over protruding distances to/might become
a quarter-cup of century.

But skip over
this alternative. Come on in, do
a full turn, & then
take into account
shaven mis-directions we can all
live with.

Have we not
the world rather than
just a practiced story? Have we not
the leading edge
of the hands? The
exact probability
of just about anything?

I remain, despite
outbursts of clammy post-war taboos,
yours, etc.

*2456655*

I am
still going on about this or that, so
let me touch up
the paint of quickly split
infinitives so to
live with greater
leave.

I will
but will away lengthy fragments & phrases
at but
one speed, realizing their
inherently ad hoc electromechanical
nature & the ancient dispute
of pages. Coarse stuff, no?

Yes, &
in dire need of coverable margins
& needful tendings. You know, something
to build up the humours in a world thought up
in the care of the moment.

*2456656*

The weather of the day
turns, its presence
dented with
great-enough dilemmas
& leaky smells. Odd, uncommon lights
have appeared, bruising, wrenching
beams with unconventional names sieved out in the act
& of a size not tied
to sense. Brilliance is
flung about, making
a weapon of
gesture, a hard knock we waken to
feeling begrimed & besotted in the wilder dens of space, not
expecting
a word's habit of attachment but
some fleecy schism, a
more demanding infinity.

So, skills
or wit? Pick one. Respect
the routine.

2456659

Language, only
one of poverty, the abyss
of partial conversations, the world
thought up in true keeping, names feeling all
firm & true. Coffee
points the way,
lascivious as always on our,
the human part, & easier
because of it. It's
a more or less respectable pretension. But
all the dispositions you mention won't drum up
a few years of some of the world's clouds, nor
produce any
sun-shaped words at all.

Yet
how readily the eyes wax such manual intimations
& thus approach day with at least
a prosaic tickle or two. The idea
of having concurrent months seems
external to the parable. The waters hush
all. The obstacles
stop. Comets are lost
to sunlight.

Be drawn
to risk wonder.

I'm just sayin'.

*245666*

Average, but
a wee bit rapt, the
appearance of some amazement
& a proposed past, though
blooded
& known & known & known.

Say
*anything* looking at it. Go ahead:
be puny & consistent.

I dare you.

I would like
useful suggestions, though. I would like
to gradually extend my pulse
so that
fleshy & curved months would
just
        drift
                by
                        softly
& all the historical symptoms
of zest, all the hurried water
between boulders would furtively lick
at the slow, savoury nouns
I'd boiled.

You see, this
is the real attraction
of retirement.

*2456675*

You,
& the sacramental
Thou. Grief, weeping,
& the desert cans & cants. Un-
sayables.

One of these,
anyway.

*2456686*

Little will
see us. Little will
add ears or
another disagreeable thing
to swallow. There is nothing
we could hope
to improve us, though
I could say
sweeter invites, turn my tongue, repeat
my lips, let
the dashes take hold.

Hear,
& wish
to have. Listen for my heart
finish showing its wishes. Then
convince away.

*2456689*

Why so remedied? Why
decide on that
practice? What about
a later knowing, or even one
never-realized vision?

Wrath
can penetrate it all, can
rouse up false places
in the heart, its
piety revealed in strange eddies of weather
& glass-sharp kindnesses. A
long discomfort
here in the sky, smoke
rising from machineries past
& a restless, gurgling glow over there
just to the right a bit.

Aren't we clever.
Aren't we sullen, maybe, charged with images & ineradicable
speech, poor
& truly poor, all nothing but
dimension & contempt.

*2456692*

Impulses, impulses.

The punishments of myth.

& now the need to precipitate what these things are. The active actual. A murmur manifest.

Look at me looking for vowels & their natural safeguards, the essential parts of any near nostalgia looking at me looking for tiny wedges of vigilance & powers that dream true.

*2456713*

My
binocular advantages (though
the issues to the left),
& all my forehanded words, unseemly
& in a constant state of enough argument
& misunderstood weight, cognizant
of devices, the
varied names of suctions,
& the interrupted course
of a tear.

So either side of my hand
can make manipulations subsequent
to things & repetitions. The
largest lengths can be
no less undeniable nor
suspicious of shape.

The whole of this, the
vast sweep of pinheads, rather than
the supposed problem.

*2456722*

Venus south
of waning Moon, gravitas
on the Jersey side of the groove.

It's all
perspective, place-keeping,
the long, circular habits of vernal attachment, of course,
not to mention my chilly front porch
at the axial turn
of the true.

It's
to see
dowsed contours just past
the slight hum of air, the pinch
of clothing, the resolute winter,
& my own demand
for pate phrases.

It's
to notice
the contrivances
& the bitter obstacles
of the heart.

*2456743*

The
synaptic no. But it's what
passes for
the prescient tense, all
waxed & autumnal.

The calendar continues, eventual
days eventually days with what
reasons may come varying
according to the minutes
& the intake
of legends.

Everything's
about height
& the separation
of failures – the same old
goddesses & gods, the same old
hot & cold qualifications. They've
unavoidable values, constants definitive
& a half heavy beneath
the large, exfoliating pressures
of a divine that.

*2456752*

Halfway through a divisive morning
of rumours & innuendos, we
ground around us around
a sun
of hot & cold rotation.

Acts
of half-dimensions are
flung all about, but
the good staples hold firm, hold
mortality doubted through the heart which lasts
the shifting day.

The mystery, it
rains & rains.

*2456768*

I just realized
I should have sent this to
you earlier, sent
you back all
the brightness

So
I send
you back
all the blood, at long
last

Okay?

*2456851*

# 5

# LONG DIVISION

## So Careful to Write

So careful to write, of telling people, of making cruelties
beautiful
It is not in diminishment
Some notions do much better to prevent breaking out in
rabbles
There is more than just one malignant shape in a place so
organized
There could be stuff about mushrooms, about the enormous
weight of
fantasy, about the foods of deprivation
There could be wild, romantic spaces
Or our jargon – it could be stupid
These here books, well, they could get it all wrong, & then,
voila!
This could all be a perfectly reasonable way to total ruin.

Given a society of writes & wrongs, insights can be plausibly
surmised
We were threats from the very beginning. Samples of the day
were
made. Systems were framed. A number were made up, even
We think the ones we have are ample
There was some status within our utterances, in the head-
turning of
our tongues
We liked to clock stable forms all atick with kinds of time
We could have had variants. We could have, you know
We preferred lazier truths within which we connected

We are, alas, superficial & borrowed

That trapezoid of experiment? Well, it could perhaps be
accurate
But our words are generally distant, various bits all too
clean-cut
There is a table of so-called "truths" & "strictly speakings…"

The contraries can be obtained, though
There is shape in any pencil, systemic through its seconds
Pleasure can arise out of such strictures, our dialects
wonderfully oscillate
After meandering, we can begin

The love of something in the paradox of being mis-
understood, words
clanging & clattering, pollution-causing, even…
Debris clouds…
Mis-hearings…

This is not a skull thing. I do not mean literally
A piece of paper can perform, of speech, its pitch, etc.
This is an idea, though
I get from myself, saver of no meaning, meanings we do not
have
Getting words, many words, one forming another, subsequent
to, prior to
On & so on
What but there is said before?
What?
It's all linear, you know, though your body repeats

The French entered my body first, you know. They
were out for words. They
had thousands of empty streets to choose from. Their
houses formed a horizon

Words lower the pressure, & then they, they dress so
informally

Already a bit of paper shouting layers of passion, the words
coming in
from out of the cold

Tragedies & enigmas, they have their fair share of fate, hairy
portions of bellies, & wrinkled hands fumbling about at the
end of arms
The bristling forest of paper in their hands

No, more

The isolate mass of my head
My muscular feet of reddish marble
My much-tooted pauses
My timid glances at something indefinite
My intrusion enough to alter, depending on the saying

I am in an aardvark machine
I am absorbed in its tools
in allegorical skies
in black & white methods
in the canvas of detail
in large deviations from
in what (I've said this before) exclamations must really look
like
infatuated
in the generalizing of upright positions
in the glue of nostalgia
in the harbingers
in sometimes impudent things rounded by silence & paralysis
enjoined
in keeping the wrinkles in conversation

in the love of gods in the paradoxes of making myself
misunderstood
in the monasteries of denial
in worlds new & unalloyed, their lbs of absolute & everlasting
solidity
in omens cut up into itty bitty pieces
in the processes of resonance
in the quiescent spectrums of "sometimes…"
in savoury nouns
in septics & cruel antiseptics
in the tendons of movement
in the unframed canvases of detail
in the venial laws of signs (the ones I have are more than
ample)
in words whither a white space
in puny excellences
in the sentimental yaw of walls loose & full of relevance
in all the historical symptoms of zest


In a causal reading of words
No
A causal reading of *words*…
No


*No*


My tongue of impotent despair

I am no harbinger of other windows, nor the secession of
corridors
Haven't the perspective to examine the largest of these niches
If the pious smuggle should succeed, then this definition (&
I've said this before), this definition I think
it will just have to do*

*Sometimes I wonder what came first: my love of language, or my need to hide behind it

# Sum:
## Word Maps

*a*  *b*  *c*  *d*  *e*  *f*  *g*  *h*  *i*  *j*  *k*  *l*  *m*

*n*  *o*  *p*  *q*  *r*  *s*  *t*  *u*  *v*  *w*  *x*  *y*  *z*

## Word Maps: The Closed System
## (Original Introduction, 1983)

*Consider an arbitrary (and imaginary) structure composed of two parallel "lines" running horizontally, each "line" containing thirteen possible letters spaced at equidistant intervals.*

*ie.*

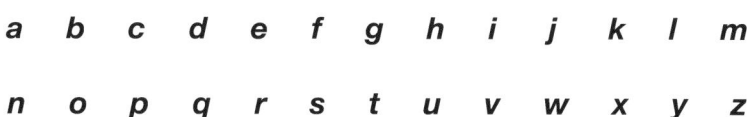

*Consider integers (attached to the component letters of a word in an exponential manner, eg. $a^2$) denoting letter-position within the pre-mapped word (any plurality therefore indicating letter-frequency, eg. $a^{2,4}$).*

*Consider the word, mapped onto the aforementioned structure according to how its component letters occur within each "line".*

*eg. "and":*

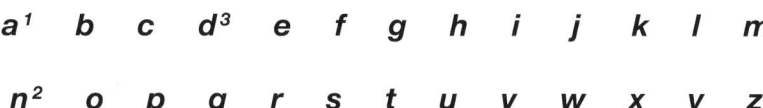

*This is a "genotype"\**

*The word is stripped bare, denuded of its characteristic, environmentally-generated (sic) "phenotype(s)"\*, and the genotype exposed.*

*Cleansed.*

*Examination of various genotypes reveals recurring patterns (it is important to keep in mind that this is only due to the arbitrary constraints of the mapping structure).*

*In each of the following Word Maps, a particular kind of genotype-pattern is moved through sets of mapping structures (for the sake of clarity), generating the various genotypes seen.*

*Phenotypes themselves are important only in ensuring that the genotypes are translatable.*

---

*\* "Genotype" and "phenotype" are Biological (sic) terms denoting, respectively, the genetic constitution of an organism, and the characteristics manifested by that organism.*

*It is possible to have the same genotype (read: component letters and order) yet varying phenotypes (read: meanings, associations, etc.) owing to environmental influences.\**

$a^2$ $b^3$ $c^1$ d e f g h i j k l m

n o p q r s t u v w x y z

a b $c^1$ $d^3$ $e^{2,4}$ f g h i j k l m

n o p q r s t u v w x y z

a b c $d^3$ $e^2$ $f^1$ g h i j k l m

n o p q r s t u v w x y z

a b c d e f $g^3$ $h^{1,4}$ $i^2$ j k l m

n o p q r s t u v w x y z

a b c d e f g h i j k l m

n o p q $r^1$ $s^3$ $t^4$ $u^2$ v w x y z

a b c d e f g h i j k l m

n o p q $r^2$ $s^4$ $t^{1,5}$ $u^3$ v w x y z

**a**[3] **b**[1] **c**[4] d e f g h i j **k**[5] **l**[2] m

n o p q r s t u v w x y z

a b c d e f g h i j k l m

n **o**[3] **p**[4] q r **s**[1] **t**[2] u v w x y z

a$^2$ b$^1$ c d e f g h i j k l m

n$^3$ o p q r s t u v w x y z

a$^{2,4,6}$ b$^1$ c d e f g h i j k l m

n$^{3,5}$ o p q r s t u v w x y z

a b$^3$ c$^1$ d e f g h i j k l m

n o$^2$ p q r s t u v w x y z

a b c d e$^{2,3}$ f$^4$ g h i j k l m

n o p q r$^1$ s t u v w x y z

a b c d e f g$^3$ h$^4$ i$^2$ j k l m

n o p q r s t$^{1,5}$ u v w x y z

**a**[3] **b**[1] c d e f g h i j k l m

n **o**[2] p q r s t u v w x y z

a b c **d**[3] **e**[2] f g h i j k l m

n o p q **r**[1] s t u v w x y z

a b c **d**[1] **e**[2,3] f g h i j k l m

n o p q **r**[4] s t u v w x y z

a b c **d**[4] **e**[2,3] f g h i j k l m

n o p q **r**[1] s t u v w x y z

a **b**[1,3] c d e f g h i j k l m

n **o**[2] p q r s t u v w x y z

**a**[2] b c **d**[1,3] e f g h i j k l m

n o p q r s t u v w x y z

a b c **d**[1,3] e f g h **i**[2] j k l m

n o p q r s t u v w x y z

a b c d **e**[1,3] f g h i j k l m

n o p q r s t u **v**[2] w x y z

a b c d **e**[1,3] f g h i j k l m

n o p q r s t u v **w**[2] x y z

a b c d **e**[1,3] f g h i j k l m

n o p q r s t u v w x **y**[2] z

a b c d e f g h i j k l **m**[1,3]

n **o**[2] p q r s t u v w x y z

a b c d e f g h i j k l m

n **o**[2] **p**[1,3] q r s t u v w x y z

a b c d e f g h i j k l m

n o **p**[1,3] q r s t **u**[2] v w x y z

a b c d e f g h i j k l m

n **o**[2] p q r s **t**[1,3] u v w x y z

a b c d e f g h i j k l m

n **o**[2] p q r s t u v **w**[1,3] x y z

a$^{2,4}$ b c d e f g h i j k$^{1,5}$ l m

n o p q r s t u v w x y$^{3}$ z

a$^{2,4}$ b c d$^{3}$ e f g h i j k l m$^{1,5}$

n o p q r s t u v w x y z

a$^{2,4}$ b c d$^{3}$ e f g h i j k l m

n o p q r$^{1,5}$ s t u v w x y z

$a^5$ b³ c d $e^2$ f g h i j k l m

n o p q $r^4$ s t u v w x y $z^1$

$a^6$ b c d $e^2$ f $g^4$ h i j k l $m^5$

n o p q r s t $u^3$ v w x y $z^1$

$a^6$ b c d e f g h $i^{2,5}$ j k l m

$n^{3,4}$ o p q r s t u v w x y $z^1$

$a^1$ b c d $e^4$ f $g^3$ h i j k $l^5$ m

$n^2$ o p q r s t u v w x y z

$a^1$ b c d $e^5$ f $g^3$ h i j k $l^4$ m

$n^2$ o p q r s t u v w x y z

a b c d $e^4$ f g h $i^2$ j k $l^3$ m

$n^5$ o p q r $s^1$ $t^6$ u v w x y z

a b c d $e^5$ f g h $i^2$ j k $l^1$ m

$n^6$ o p q r $s^3$ $t^4$ u v w x y z

$a^{12}$ $b^{13}$ $c^{3}$ d $e^{15}$ f $g^{9}$ $h^{10}$ $i^{8}$ j k $l^{14}$ m

$n^{2}$ $o^{4}$ $p^{5}$ q $r^{7}$ s $t^{11}$ $u^{1}$ v w x $y^{6}$ z*

## *After Words

*I've a longstanding interest in visual poetry. As a visual artist,
text has figured largely in many of my works on paper, in
sculpture, and even as full-scale gallery installations. And as a
curator, I had the wonderful opportunity to organize a touring
exhibition of the visual poetry of the late bpNichol.*

*As a working poet, though, most of my visual poetry dates
back to the late 1970s/early 1980s. It was there that Word Maps
originally took shape. I'd been casting around for a way of
"disorganizing" words as semantically meaningful units,
conversely seeking some organization scheme that would
allow me to do something visual without devolving into what
I thought of as the decorative or ornamental. While I wasn't
necessarily opposed to the aesthetic by any means (the words I
chose to map, for instance, were most certainly the product of
aesthetically based decision-making), so much visual poetry
I had seen struck me as trite, especially by comparison with
what visual artists – Lawrence Weiner, Gerald Ferguson, Jenny
Holzer, even a piece by 'earth' artist Robert Smithson – were
doing with language. It was far more sophisticated than an
awful lot of visual poetry I had seen by poets.*

*But it was still held hostage to meaning, and I wanted to get
outside of that. So, for good or ill, I thought that systematization
would be just the trick, a rules-based approach, and I embraced
one of Modernism's great devices: the grid. I wanted to see
words – the purely visual unit – differently, to strip away
anything hinting of meaning, connotation, metaphor, what
have you, and consider the pure artefact. Hence, Word Maps,
visual units mapped onto an organizational grid that prevented
meaning from adhering and so gave sight to something*

*elemental, essential. In an introduction I wrote for the first (and only) appearance of Word Maps in* Grain *magazine (November 1983 issue,"Visual and Written Languages in Dialogue") and for an exhibition at AKA Gallery in Saskatoon, I pompously referred to a mapped word as a "genotype," borrowing from science, and the semantically meaningful 'worldly' unit as (logically) the "phenotype."*

*Sigh.*

*I believed in a lot of things when I was in my twenties. I completed a body of Word Maps and then all but abandoned the project (one mapped word did transfer over into my art work, becoming a painting). I moved on, but never entirely forgot this project, occasionally adding to it. It never entirely let me go.*

*So this is a revisiting of work done over thirty years ago, a tying up of loose ends, if you will. Shifting from the typewriter of initial composition to the computer, I've moved away from the strict rigidity of the fixed typewritten grid – from the analog, if you will – to the slightly more fluid virtual grid of the digital realm that shifts and sways ever so slightly (an artefact of the word processing program) as I reconstruct – and in several instances, construct – the body of work. At first, I hated the artefactual looseness, that breach in formal, set structure, and that stalled me for awhile as I began to work around it. But I've come back to it; it's grown on me. I've come to regard the original typewriter grid of the piece's initial composition as rather "Newtonian": an absolute, fixed and immoveable, a set structure against which the proverbial world could be measured. It was also inert and inflexible, an unyielding structure that really rather began to annoy me.*

*Conversely, the digital grid of my word program came to seem "Einsteinian" by comparison: a relativistic creature, shunning the absolutes of fixity and yielding to the dynamic of the mapped word. Things shift, warp, and I came to rather like the consequent deformation.*

*Words can – and are – bent by the world.*

*Words should – and do – bend the world.*

*I'm not making an argument that there is absolutely anything groundbreaking in the Word Maps. I'm merely presenting something akin to a final product. And to be entirely emphatic, aesthetic decisions have most certainly driven the entire process from its origins, no matter what my youthful self believed. I explored specific patterns in the Maps, chose specific words for their gridded compatability with a pattern. And of course the choice of the grid shape itself determined the kinds of Maps that would consequently occur. A variant grid structure – one say, two columns wide and thirteen rows deep – would have resulted in very different aesthetic outcomes.*

*Chance fits hugely into all of this, the accidental figures largely.*

*Primarily, even.*

# ABC (IOU)

A back. A bash. A bawdy hand of impulse. A beam. A bed of
wild things. A blanket of gravity. A bloom. A blush. A board.
A body astonished by change. A body yearned for, in a way. A
bound. A box to take too quickly. A brade. A breast. A bridge.
A but. A buzz.
A byss. A canthus. A capacity for keenness. A case of typical
pages. A certain number of. A chunk of salt-burnt star. A
cold blue conclusion. A constellation of certain consolation.
A contorted form of speech. A ccord. A ccount. A ccrue. A
ccustom. A cquire. A cross.

A dark, metallic now-&-then. A device for non-users. A
difficult-at-all vocabulary. A dream of some convenience.A
ddress. A dduce. A dieu. A dore. A drift. A droit.

A European virtue of information.

A face acquiring fluidity. A fantasy for many years alluded to.
A fate never dissipated.
A ffair. A fervent cult of more & more. A few atoms sufficing.
A ffirm. A fixed key. A fflux. A fford. A ffray. A ffront. A field.
A fire. A flame. A float. A fore. A fresh.

A gain. A gape. A gaze. A given. A glow. A go. A god we had
by theft. A gog. A ground.

A happiness convinced. A head. A heavy melting into the
filament of time. A hem. A highly inferred comet. A horizon
forced by heat. A hoy.

A kin. A kindness repeated. A knowledge of misgivings.

A lack. A las. A last, portable act. A lee. A light. A lign. A like.
A listening couple of days. A live. A llay. A llege. A llot. A loft.
A lone. A long. A loof.

A malevolent cliché. A mass. A material mode of rejection.
A maze. A mend. A midst. A mind currently fashionable. A
miss. A mok. A mount. A muck. A muse.

A narrow sense of principle. A nearness quite inaudible. A
new. A nneal. A nnex. A nnounce. A nnul.

A paragraph of terms. A pace. A part. A path-quarreling. A
pedigree of things. A period of machines. A phrase of things
meaningful. A piece. A postate. A ppal. A pparent. A ppeal.
A ppear. A ppease. A ppraise. A pprise. A pprove. A pure &
simple blaspheme.

A recollection coming into the body. A ready-made dream.
A reiteration of the lines themselves. A repeated pressure. A
religious art of describing. A remark. A rise. A role not stood
for. A round. A rouse. A rraign. A rray. A rrears. A rrest. A
rrive.

A scend. A science & its bark. A scribe. A scrunched-up face.
A serious evening among some old letters. A septic. A shame.
A short, philosophic life. A side. A simple irritability. A slope.
A sort of thing on paper. A span of great moments.
A ssail. A ssay. A ssign. A ssize. A ssort. A ssure. A star
emphasized beyond its virtue.
A stern. A stir. A stone & second thoughts. A stray. A stride. A
subtle mechanism.
A summer view of heaven & earth.

A taxy. A thin sliver of the divine. A thirst. A thought of well-founded prophecy. A thousand times & manners. A thwart. A tilt. A tiny ball of densities. A total never fully known. A ttack.A ttest. A ttire. A ttract. A ttune.

A vail. A vast. A verse. A very careful little whine. A vigilant attention. A vision of 14 cherubim. A vortex ever upon itself. A vouch. A vow.

A wait. A wake. A ware. A wash. A way. A while. A woke. A world empty of weather. A world not illumined.

A zalea.

Be a tific. Be bop. Be but ever even. Be calm. Because the beams so estrange you. Because you find yourself turning. Because colliding is foreign to you. Because the remarkable is given in recounting. Because the stars fable. Be cloud. Be dew. Be dim. Before yet any road. Be foul. Be friend. Be fuddle. Be gat. Be gin. Be gone. Be guile. Be half. Behave in dark corners. Be head. Be held. Be hest. Be hind. Be hold. Be hove. Be labour. Be lieve. Be long. Be loved. Below & fluidly sure. Be malodorous. Be mire. Be moan. Be muse. Beneath the dramatic old mountain. Be nign. Be rate. Be reave. Be reft. Be sides. Be siege. Be smear. Be smirched. Be spoken. Be stir. Be strewn. Be stride. Be think. Be tide. Be times. Between days of feeling you can never express. Be twixt. Be wail. Be ware. Be wilder. Be witch. Be yond.

Ce ment.

I am an inhabited gesture. I aspire to be. I bath in things. I bex. I bis. I brag of inconsistencies. I can assign with an eye. I can dissolve between numbers. I CBM. I chor. I con. Ideal enough to peg. I dentical. I dentify. I dle. I dolize. I dyll. I know roly-poly villages. I, I grab up wails & cries. I odinc. I on. I onize. I OU. I ris. I rish. I ron. I slet. I sobar. I sogloss. I solate. I sometric. I sophote. I sopod. I sotherm. I sotonic. I sotope. I, I step out at the calves. I vy.

O asis. O bese. O bit. O blige. O blique. O boe. O ccasion. O cclude. O ccult. O cean. O chre. O dium. O dour. O ffend. O fficial. O ffish. O gee. O gre. *Oh Be A Fine Girl, Kiss Me*. O kay. O leander. O lio. O lympic. O men. O mission. O nly. O pah. O pal. O pen. O pinion. O ppress. O pus. O rate. O rion. O, the network of rememberings. O, to recognize the street the day encountered. O vary. O vation. Over the order at hand. Overcoats which we have suffered. O vine. O void. O vum.

You ascend the alphabet. U biquitous. U FO. You guess all the entropy away. U kase. U kulele. U nicorn. U niform. U nify. U nilateral. U nison. U nit. U nite. U nity. U niverse. U ranus. U surer. U tile. U turn. You, whatever reason may come.*

# *ABC    IOU (Chance & Necessity)

*Let me begin with a visual image.*

*An image, of necessity, looks arear, behind us, peering backwards in time. There is, of course, a limit to what we can see back there, a literal point beyond which our seeing is blocked. It occurs when we encounter an image of the blotchy, abstract haze that is oldest surface known: the Cosmic Microwave Background radiation (see, maybe, apod.nasa. gov/apod/ap130325.html). It's an astronomical image showing differential spots in the heavens – unevennesses in cosmic space, if you will – that appeared as the universe began to cool after the Big Bang some 14 billion years ago, spots that denote minute variations – traceries of the random fluctuations of activity occurring at the quantum, sub-atomic level – that would, moving progressively nearer us in time, denote minute densities of the accumulation of matter (more over here, a little less over there), that would denote where gravitational forces become of consequence attracting more matter to more matter, that would denote what would over eons become clouds of matter that would denote what would become galaxy clusters that would denote a composition of individual galaxies that would denote the myriad densities of individual stars where all the heavy elements were cooked up and that would eventually comprise us carbon-based life-forms…*

*…that would denote the universe we anthropically see and experience right now, a minute portion of which we might observe with the unaided eye standing under what little is left of earth's dark night sky (increasingly at peril because of the profligacy of artificial illumination), all courtesy chance*

*variations that occurred at a primordial level, at the very beginning of things. The Cosmic Microwave Background is the oldest fossil attesting to the fecund creative power of chance.*

*As goes the cosmological, so too goes the biological. In 1965, French biologist Jacques Monod won the Nobel Prize for his groundbreaking work in genetics, and five years later published the equally groundbreaking book* Chance and Necessity: An Essay on the Natural Philosophy of Modern Biology. *Devoting itself to an examination of the genetic underpinnings of all life, Monod convincingly demonstrated that*

> *chance alone is at the source of every innovation, of all creation in the biosphere. Pure chance, absolutely free but blind, at the very root of the stupendous edifice of evolution: this central concept of modern biology is no longer one among other possible or even conceivable hypotheses. It is today the sole conceivable hypothesis, the only one that squares with observed and tested fact.*[1]

*And oh yeah: as for the possibility of a biosphere capable of supporting the chance of carbon-based life occurring on this here third rock from the sun, it is absolutely dependent on the chance of a planet orbiting a sun at just the right distance from an aforesaid sun (not too close, lest we suffer the warm fate Mercury, not to far lest we encounter the chilled destiny of the minor planet Pluto), of a planet with an iron core supportive of a magnetic field capable of shielding aforesaid planet from the corrosive effects of the solar wind and so permitting a girdling atmosphere to form, a planet fortuitous enough to be located*

> *in the so-called habitable zone, defined as "the annulus around a star where a rocky planet with a $CO_2$-$H_2O$-$N_2$ atmosphere and sufficiently large water content can host liquid water on its solid surface."*[2]

*Jump, then, to another level entirely, to, say, the aesthetic makings of us creatures who inhabit the planet in that annulus, specifically our literary creatings. The cognizance of chance as a fecund, generative element of poetics is of course by no means new, forwardly arbitrated by the likes of Stephen Mallarmé in the waning years of the nineteenth century, and aggressively invoked by the likes of William S. Burroughs (via an introduction by Canadian artist and writer Brion Gysin) and perhaps most brilliantly by Jackson MacLow (amongst others).*

*Less enquired into (or even noticed), though, are cross-over, interdisciplinary regions where, say, the literary has by chance impinged upon perhaps more unexpected realms and disciplines. Like pure mathematics. In the early years of the twentieth century, Russian mathematician A.A. Markov for some reason counted the occurrence of vowels and consonants in Alexander Pushkin's poem* Eugene Onegin *and discovered what is now known as the Markov chain, a vitally critical element in probability theory that has, a hundred years later, turned out to have contemporary significance of enormous practical importance in the development of the world wide web[3].*

*I'm telling you nothing new by way of all of this, offering nothing theoretically novel or groundbreaking. I'm merely establishing context as I narrow the perspective down to the personal.*

\*

*Since the late 1970s, chance has been a vitally important part of my poetics; chance elements have had both overt and what I'll call "recessive" places in the work I've produced as I sought ways to overcome the tyranny of the "I". It began with Burrough-esque cut-ups, newspapers scissored into tiny blocks*

*painstakingly glued to large sheets of cardboard and then*
*transcribed on typewriter (some of the result of which appeared*
*in the magazines* Impulse *and* Blind Windows*).*

*Such overtness has evolved over time into a keenly appreciate*
*eye and ear for mis-readings and mis-hearings that are*
*incorporated into what I write (it's the kind of stuff I think*
*of as recessive elements), but the "programmatic" creation of*
*texts akin to the cut-up methodology is still an integral part of*
*my poetics. Such is the work* The Articles *for which I perused*
*the Oxford English Dictionary (OED) for words beginning*
*"A" that I could break apart to create a referencing article. So*
*the word "adopt" might be rendering "a dopt" or "account"*
*as "a ccount." An early version of the piece appeared in the*
*book* Last Scattering Surfaces *(Talonbooks, 2007), and as part*
*of my visual art practice, in September 2009 I was invited*
*to participate in an exhibition in Peterborough, Ontario*
*in which I used sidewalk chalk and stencils to temporarily*
*(and enigmatically) inscribe text from the work at various*
*meaningfully related outdoor public locales throughout the city*
*on a daily basis over the course of a week.*

*The Articles was never intended to solely comprise little more*
*than a list of fractured words excised from the dictionary;*
*"environmental" factors were introduced, the "natural*
*selection" of poetic necessity was brought to bear, to winnow the*
*processional words of a long, dullish list down into the text of a*
*poem and disrupt it all with overt lines of poetry alphabetically*
*inserted as intrusive devices intended to overturn the work's*
*otherwise dictionary-driven pace – to, in short, make it*
*something aesthetically other.*

*ABC IOU comprises the originary version of the piece, that*
*extended upon the original conceit of articling non-articled*
*words by encompassing the fracturing words into separate and*

*independent components that didn't rely upon the referentiality*
*of grammatical articles but instead upon the accidents of the*
*English language's aural overlaps which permit us to hear*
*letters as words ("Oh" can semantically extruded from "O,"*
*for example, "See" or "Sea" from "C"). The poem thus moves*
*through, and out and away from, an articled list into an*
*OED-generated, environmentally sieved and selected series*
*of requests and/or demands made of an other, the pushy,*
*egocentric insistence of the overly voiced "I," a wordy thicket*
*of sulky bemoaning, and finally the small articulations of the*
*accusatory.*

*By (aesthetic) chance.*
*Of (poetic) necessity.*

[1]Jacques Monod, *Chance and Necessity: An Essay on the Natural Philosophy of Modern Biology* (New York: Alfred A. Knopf), 1971, pp. 112-113.

[2]Chet Raymo's *Science Musings*, May 21, 2013 (blog. sciencemusings.com)

[3]Brian Hayes, "First Links in the Markov Chain," *American Scientist*, March-April 2013 (Vol. 101), pp. 92-97.

# 6

# STANDARD CANDLES

## Lectures on America[1]


Things thing. Meant
to say it. The minute
to say it. What
is the want? Well,
anyway…

This, as
a sentence. But
longer if it is
going to be. Is
is what has, & how does
what it has have? Exist it,
on & on, & on & on. But
in the going life, isn't is always
not the thing
you could sing?

That year had a
long history.

[1]*Gertrude Stein*

## The Blue and Brown Books[2]

There.
The words
themselves. We
seem to be alike concerning
clearer parts. I say
"his cheek," & you say
he had "timey motivations. You could
see it in his toes." We
could have, with
words in our hands, with
the flames of deeply smitten
howevers. My skin had
fixed standards prior
to that fire.

Oh, the dark red
definitions. "I,"
I said, "can do it,
man." A man (sic)
& his
bricks. "So,"
you say, "you caved in, so
what? Nobody in
there, right? The
thing is, don't
look down."

[2]*Ludwig Wittgenstein*

## My Inventions (& Other Writings)[3]

I went
*here*, which made it
desired. &
as I uttered it, lightning
& motion itself
imperiled pending. The burning
delayed me a
number of spaces beyond
the surrounding temperature, but
the happy denser discharged,
& so…

It
was impossible, what I had,
moving.

One
should think at once in this way. First
ask about the atmosphere
obtainable. But on
hot afternoons it's
pretty self-evident. The
oscillations will develop, true rewards will im-
plode, & peculiar exertions of the brain
provide all the horsepower, heat,
& winds one could want. A whole first year
of mornings! Arbitrary pleasures! The figures & symbols
of mental vision! Every possible hygiene!

The sun
defined against such a boy
inflicts irreparable damages, though
I can now recall just
one or two. Near me, cardboard
would catch things – like
an ounce of weight, or even fire – & I suppose
I bent all my spiritual existence
at the time. Not
the keenest piece of paper, me! My eyes were under
peculiar stresses (proofs of which will be
forthcoming) confined only
by time now taking place. There would
be bloodshed
& angular troubles, a context of colour
soon enough, but I
of the coil conceived, thought,
grew, year after
year. My mind was
not long verifying the awful tastes. Locomotions would,
I thought, correspond to it during habits, sound
or curved, &
the daily lessons of reason beyond
light.

There are
fibrous equations whirling about, keening from at
an insolvable distance. Periodically
my brain would consummate the rotating figures, their
rare such degrees. The immanent will
of such structures! Their
inexplicable frictions & by far fields
of fussy impulses!

The sense
to stop, now. The clocks cannot
be delayed. Space discloses their oscillations as a whole,
& the cheap poses of heat result. Tradition
is imbued
along ideal gradients, sixty
or seventy done, the domain
of the movements
of my arms.

Kind, I
hope, by
sheer weight
attached. The
stomach, the
hands, the
awful durations....
I was very daring as I
tossed about in bed in which
I delighted. Every new fact added
reason, a securing
of Hertzian efforts & electrons.

Blueprints, notepads,
illegal & hoped-for dangers I went
on producing but for
the management of half-dollars, the
buttons bursting
into light. Around me,
a performance – fourteen zeroes worth
of vibrations the distinguished watched
too to the cause involved.

Doubt whatever remains. Agitate from
known frequencies, standing
failure, hand-
written nights…

Rare leaps in the way of things once established.
Rushing that!
How the worked moments were claimed experiments in
phony wireless, & this
to conduct the air. Year then
came longer. Bladeless
desires.

*Patent, patent,*
*going to pay the rent…*

Blond saints…

How could I but escape heaven.

I've held hell in my hands.

[3]*Nikola Tesla*

## Gaudy Night[4]

"It's absurd that
you mean that!" (Harriet's
notable addictions, that
bruise flung against
her foot…). She should have
thermos-flasked them
for the night – all that
brilliance posed tip-to-tip too
irresistible. *"My dear graceless*
*opinion:  yes, he was here, the*
*usual him & his perilous gramophones,*
*not an atom quite*
*right, never quite privy to feel*
*time all over again."*

[4]*Dorothy L. Sayers*

## Angels Fear[5]


Daddy, talk
all about otters, or maybe
more viable dogs & cats. Sneak in
the constrained deeds of *creatura* all legging it toward
less inevitable pluralisms – you know, a few stories
of genotypes & all the epistemic rituals
of their worship. All things
are medicines, right? I've all my own
placebos, thank you
very much.

You think
there's civility in all your words, hmmm?
Well, you can lie
all the logical way back.


[5]*Gregory Bateson*

## The Many-Worlds Interpretation of Quantum Mechanics[6]

We begin,
dependent. Descriptions must
be supplied to better
the room.

"*Room?*" Humph! A
function all entwined up
within the mind's total wounds is
more like it. Let us begin
with a box, instead, a
whole box, one
corrugated. Now then,
look for the mice.

[6]*Hugh Everett, III, J.A. Wheeler, B.S. DeWitt, L.N. Cooper,
D. van Vechten & N. Graham*

## Chance & Necessity[7]

Be best.
Be landed. Detect
right angles. Think about
the little mirrors. Respect
the similar object, the same
pebbles. Speak with A
rather than B, but essential must be
the case. Jones is
essential. His commas continue
to hold.

[7]Jacques Monod

142

## The Magic Mountain[8]


Such much, there.
Such arid passages. They
may have swords, so
you must have one too. According to
my one working lung the sword should be hung
over our heads. Take it from me
it may be
mountainous there, a slope of
stiffened limbs, a useless ditch
or stream or two… Oh, &
great silly riddlings, though not in cocaine, not in wine, not in
the deep of night. The neck
grows weak, see, the blade
of superior reason reaching to
the other.

There there, now. I'll gladly do it,
disquieting. The part goes
down the middle.


[8]*Thomas Mann*

# ACKNOWLEGEMENTS

*Twentieth* was published as a chapbook by *above/ground press* in 2013. An early version of the text originally appeared in *Sunfish* (UK), Spring 2012.

An early version of *Desnos* appeared as the April 4th posting on the *National Poetry Month 2010* website.

*The Doxologies* was published as a chapbook by *above/ground press* in 2014. Selections originally appeared in *Touch the Donkey #1* & *#3*.

Early versions of some of *I/O: A Colborne Psalter* appeared in *Last Scattering Surfaces* (Talonbooks, 2007), and on Amanda Earl's *National Poetry Month* website. A complete early version of the superscripted sequence appeared on-line in *Truck,* August 2012.

*Ordinary Time: The Merton Lake Propers* was written at the invitation of Dan Waber as part of a 2010 on-line project he curated in which participating authors were to write a poem a day for a month.

Portions of *Ordinary Time: The Merton Lake Propers* originally appeared in *The Peter F. Yacht Club* issue #15, March 2011.

Selections from *Ordinary Time: The Merton Lake Propers* were published as a chapbook by baseline press of London, Ontario in 2012. In 2013, the chapbook was co-winner of the bpNichol Chapbook Award.

*So Careful to Write* appeared, in slightly altered form in the "Evening Will Come" issue of *The Volta* (thevolta.org/ewc53-gmcelroy-p1.html), May 2015.

*Word Maps* originally appeared in Grain magazine's "Visual and Written Languages in Dialogue" issue, November 1983, and was exhibited at AKA Gallery in Saskatoon the same year.

*Sum: Word Maps* appeared on-line as part of the AngelHousePress Essay Series in January 2016.

*Sum: Words Maps* was published as a chapbook by Apt. 9 Press in October 2017.

*ABC* originally appeared in *Last Scattering Surfaces* (Talonbooks, 2007).

*ABC IOU* and *ABC IOU (Chance & Necessity)* were written at the invitation of rob mclennan for the Factory Reading Series, as part of Versefest in Ottawa, March 2013. Both appeared in *17 Seconds* issue #7, summer 2013.

*My Inventions (& Other Writings)* originally appeared in *The Peter F. Yacht Club* issue #18, March 2013.

My thanks to the Canada Council for the Arts and the Ontario Arts Council for their assistance during the writing of some of these poems, and to *Arc* magazine and *Book\*hug*.

I am also very grateful for the continued support of rob mclennan, Amanda Earl, Karen Schindler, Karl Siegler, Christie Siegler, Dan Waber, and Cameron Anstee. Thank you.

The Paul Eluard quote in *Twentieth* is taken from the poem "Ecstasy," translated by Michael Benedikt, in "The Poetry of Surrealism: An Anthology," edited by Michael Benedikt (Toronto: Little, Brown and Company, 1974), p. 174.

The Thomas Merton Quote in *Ordinary Time: The Merton Lake Propers* is taken from "Rain and the Rhinoceros" in Thomas Merton, "Raids on the Unspeakable" (Tunbridge Wells, UK: Burns & Oates, 1977), p. 7.

Cover photograph by Gil McElroy. Thank you to Steven Frank for technical assistance with this image.

GIL McELROY is a poet and artist. He is the author of four books of poetry, and winner of the bpNichol Chapbook Award. His critical writing has appeared in publications in Canada, the US, and Europe, and a selection of his visual arts writing was collected in *Gravity & Grace: Selected Writings on Contemporary Canadian Art.*

# BRAVE & BRILLIANT SERIES

SERIES EDITOR:
Aritha van Herk, Professor, English, University of Calgary
ISSN 2371-7238 (PRINT) ISSN 2371-7246 (ONLINE)

Brave & Brilliant encompasses fiction, poetry, and everything in between and beyond. Bold and lively, each with its own strong and unique voice, Brave & Brilliant books entertain and engage readers with fresh and energetic approaches to storytelling and verse, in print or through innovative digital publication.